·Contents·

A Brownie box camera and case, 1900.

Some of the more difficult words appear in the text in **bold**.
These words are explained in the picture glossary on page 28.
The pictures will help you to understand the entries more easily.

Oxford Street is a busy street in London.

There are buses and taxis on the road.
The surface of the street is made of tarmac.
Traffic lights, signs and **road markings** help to direct drivers.
People walk on wide **pavements**.

Oxford Street was busy 100 years ago.

Most **vehicles** at this time were pulled by horses.

There were no traffic lights and few road signs.

The road was made of **cobble stones** set close together.

This shop is in a special street where cars cannot go.

Some towns have shopping areas where the streets
are mainly for **pedestrians**.
Delivery vans or lorries are allowed in the street
at special times of the day.
Pedestrianized streets like this are safer for shoppers.

Streets were not as busy as today.

There was less traffic on the roads.

The car had only just been invented and vehicles moved more slowly.

Most people walked or cycled to work and to the shops.

This is a typical corner shop.

The owner sells sweets, groceries, newspapers and many other things. Most of the customers live near the shop. Many families prefer to drive to a supermarket to do their shopping.

There was a general store in most large streets.

This kind of shop sold many different things, but most other shops at this time were small and sold one type of **goods**.

Some towns have a market in the main street.

The **stalls** are put up early in the morning and taken down at night.
Traffic has to be directed along other roads.
In many places the market has been moved to a special site
away from the busy streets.

Most towns and villages had a street market.

The market was held in the main street every week.

People travelled into the town from the countryside on Market Day.

They did their shopping and met their friends.

This street trader sells ice-cream from a van.

Music plays to tell people that the ice-cream seller is in the street.
The driver stops the van to sell ice-cream.
Then he drives on to the next street.

Ice-cream was sold from hand carts in the street.

Many different kinds of food could be bought in the streets.
Traders shouted to let people know what they could buy.
Many children worked as street sellers.

Dave and Rob play music in the street.

This is called busking.

Buskers entertain people in the street and can be found in many towns.

People stop to listen and give them money.

There were different kinds of entertainers in the street.

Street organs were popular.

Music played when a handle on the organ was turned and the monkeys danced and collected money from the audience.

Street entertainers moved from one street to another.

Post boxes are found in many streets.

Most are made of iron and painted red. Some post boxes are a hundred years old. Post boxes, **litter** bins, signs and bus shelters are all things found in the street.

There were
post boxes
in the street
100 years
ago.

The first post box
was put up in 1852.
It had six sides and
was made of iron.

Michael delivers newspapers.

People pay the **newsagent** to have papers and
magazines brought to their homes.
Sometimes newspapers are sold from stands in the street.

This man sold newspapers in the street.

Customers stopped him when they wanted to buy a paper.
Many different goods were brought to homes by delivery boys
riding bicycles with large baskets fixed to the front.

This man is a street cleaner.

People and traffic make the streets dirty and untidy.

Special machines are used to pick up the rubbish.

Dirt and litter are sucked up from the road into the machine.

Street cleaners worked with brushes and **shovels**.

Streets in towns were often dirty and muddy.
Women with long skirts had to be careful as they walked across the road.

There are road-works in this street.

The street is being re-surfaced.

Busy roads are damaged and worn out by traffic.

Potholes and cracks appear in the road surface.

Most of the repair work is done by machines.

Many new roads were built.

The invention of the petrol engine meant that more vehicles travelled on the roads.

More roads were needed to link the new houses being built.

Men did most of the work by hand.

These men are mending a street light.

Street lighting makes roads safer for pedestrians and traffic.
The lights are electric and switch on and off automatically.
Street lights have to be checked and repaired regularly.

The streets in many towns were lit by gas lamps.

Lamplighters lit the gas in the street lamps when it got dark.
In the morning they turned off the gas and the light went out.
Some of the bigger houses had gas lighting too.

Parents watch their children in the playground.

Today the traffic makes streets dangerous for children.

Boys and girls can be knocked down on the roads.

Playgrounds give children a safe place to play away from cars, lorries and other traffic.

Children often played in the street.

There was less traffic so many children used the streets as their playground.
Vehicles were slower and more noisy, but it was still dangerous
to play in the street.

· Picture Glossary ·

 **cobble stones** Stones with round edges that were used to make the surface of roads.

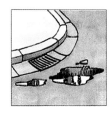 **pothole** A hole in a road.

 **goods** Things to sell.

 **road markings** Lines, arrow and other signs painted on the road to help drivers.

 **litter** Empty packets, cartons and paper dropped on the street by people.

 **shovels** Types of spade, mad of metal and sometimes with a wooden handle.

 **newsagent** A shopkeeper who sells or delivers newspapers, magazines and comics.

 **stalls** Special stands used by market traders to display the goods they have to sell.

 **pavements** Flat areas by the side of the road, used for people to walk on away from the traffic.

 **traffic lights** Lights placed where busy roads meet. Red, amber and green lights mean that drivers stop, wait or go.

 **pedestrians** People who walk along a street.

 **vehicles** Cars, buses, lorries and other types of transport with wheels.

· Books to Read ·

The Past in Pictures: The Victorians by John Malam (Wayland, 2006)
Who Lived Here? My Victorian Home, My 1930's Home and *My 1950's Home* by Karen Bryant-Mole (Watts, 2006)
What was it like in the Past? series: *At School* and *In the Street* by Louise and Richard Spilsbury. *On Journeys* and *At Home* by Mandy Ross (Heinemann Library, 2006)
What is it like Now? series: *At Home, On Journeys* and *At School* by Tony Pickford (Heinemann Library, 2006)

· Places to Visit ·

Many local museums have collections or displays depicting life in the street. It is worth contacting them to see what they can offer.
The following examples are specialist museums.

Preston Hall Museum,
Yarm Road,
Stockton-on-Tees, TS18 3RH

  Telephone: 01642 781184

Blist Hill Victorian Town
Ironbridge,
Telford,
Shropshire, TF8 7AW

  Tel: 01952 844391

The Cregneash Village Folk Museum,
Port St. Mary,
Isle of Man

  Tel: 01624 648000

New Lanark World Heritage Site
South Lanarkshire,
Scotland, ML11 9DB

  Tel: 01555 661345

The Shambles Museum
  (Small Victorian Town)
16-24 Church Street,
Newent,
Gloucestershire, GL8 1PP

  Tel: 01531 822144

Lark Hill Place,
Salford Museum and Art Gallery,
Peel Park,
The Crescent,
Salford, M5 4WU

  Tel: 0161 778 0820

The Black Country Museum,
Tipton Road,
Dudley,
West Midlands

  Tel: 0121 557 9643

Further Information about the Photographs

PHOTOGRAPH ON PAGE 5 **Oxford Street, 1909.**

About this photograph

Horse-drawn buses provided their own form of traffic congestion and there were no road markings to help traffic flow. The photograph shows the formal nature of shopping in the capital. Nearly everyone is wearing a hat and some of the ladies' hats look very grand. The problem of walking along dirty streets in long skirts is indicated by the lady in the front of the photograph who is raising her skirt to walk properly.

Questions to ask

What sort of clothes are people wearing to go shopping?
How do you think shoppers took their purchases home?
What sounds do you think you would hear in this street?

Points to explore

Transport – horse-drawn buses, carriages, cars.
Street markings – directional, warning, giving orders, informational.
Street surfaces – manhole covers, grids, drains.

PHOTOGRAPH ON PAGE 7 **Boots the Chemist, 1916.**

About this photograph

The shop window takes up the major part of this photograph and displays a variety of different items for sale inside the shop. Boots is a good example of a modern store which has its origins in the nineteenth century. The photograph shows how shop entrances were smaller than today. Shoppers here would come straight from the street into the shop.

Questions to ask

What sort of shop is this and what does it sell?
What advantages does a traffic-free street have for shoppers?
How do the goods get into the shops?

Points to explore

Printing – shop and street signs, advertising.
Shop windows – display, window dressing, shapes of windows.
Street furniture – poles, lights, benches, litter bins.

PHOTOGRAPH ON PAGE 9 **General Stores, 1910.**

About this photograph

The photograph shows a general store with a variety of goods for sale. By 1900 department stores were growing up in the larger cities. Some of these, such as the Army and Navy Stores, were co-operatives, but others were privately owned. In smaller towns shops were still locally owned and many of the goods would be ordered and delivered later.

Questions to ask

What sort of things do you think this general store would sell?

Points to explore

Growth of supermarkets and out of town shopping, demise of small specialist shops.
Survey of local shops – goods sold, size, type.

PHOTOGRAPH ON PAGE 11 **Chrisp Street Market in Poplar London, 1904.**

About this photograph

This is a fairly typical street market showing a large number of stalls offering different goods for sale. In large towns stall holders were likely to be the middle-men, but in smaller towns and villages they were the men, women and children who had grown or made the goods. Markets were important for bringing people into the towns and villages from outlying areas.

Questions to ask

What sort of goods are being sold?
What are the stalls made from and how permanent are they?
What problems might this street market cause?

Points to explore

People – age, gender, clothes, pose.
Street – surface, signs, buildings.

PHOTOGRAPH ON PAGE 13 **Ice-cream man at St. Clement Dane Church, 1912.**

About this photograph

This is an example of a street trader doing a good trade in ice-creams despite the fact that the photograph was taken in January. Throughout the eighteenth and nineteenth centuries, in London and other large cities, there were thousands of itinerant vendors, including many children. Nursery rhymes such as Do you know the Muffin Man? and Hot Cross Buns grew from this sort of activity.

Questions to ask

Where do you think the boys are going?
What sort of weather do you think it was when the photograph was taken? How do you know?

Points to explore

Local street traders and mobile shops.
Hygiene – traffic dust and fumes, washing facilities, litter.

PHOTOGRAPH ON PAGE 15 **Monkeys on a Street Organ, 1903.**

About this photograph

Street entertainment like this was an important form of recreation for the poor. There were musicians, acrobats and singers. Animals were used to entertain as well. The photograph shows the clothes of working class children around the turn of the century. They were dressed for hard wear and tear. Some of the girls had smocks to protect their dresses from dirt and dust. The boys' clothes were made of corduroy or tweed and nearly everyone is wearing a hat.

Questions to ask

Why does this street entertainer have monkeys on the organ?
How does he make money?
How would the organ be moved from one place to another?

Points to explore

Clothing – hats, smocks.
Other kinds of street entertainment.

PHOTOGRAPH ON PAGE 17 **Postman in the Street, Isle of Man, 1900.**

About this photograph

Apart from the uniform, this photograph could almost be contemporary. Post boxes were first established in 1852. The collections were arranged to fit in with the times of the trains which carried the main mails. The design of the boxes has changed over the years and the monarch's initials provide a possible way of dating both the pillar box and the creation of the street.

Questions to ask

How do you know this photograph was not taken today?
What initials do local post boxes have on them?
Whose initials are they?

Points to explore

Postman's uniform – similarities and differences between a modern postal worker's uniform.
Other items of street furniture.

PHOTOGRAPH ON PAGE 19 **Church Army Worker on 'Two-Penny-Farthing', 1890.**

About this photograph

Delivery boys were a familiar sight in streets and many goods were delivered in this way. This may partly explain why photographs taken of Victorian and Edwardian streets rarely show people carrying their shopping. However, a close look at this photograph suggests it was taken as an advertisement for the Church Army. The boy in the background is reading the Church Army paper and the young man appears to be delivering it.

Questions to ask

What job do you think this man does?
How does he steer the tricycle?

Points to explore

Bicycles and tricycles – bicycling clubs, opening up of the countryside to a greater number of people through cheap transport. Some of the problems of riding a bicycle – then (surface of roads) and now (broken glass on streets, heavy traffic).

PHOTOGRAPH ON PAGE 21 **A Road Sweeper, 1902.**

About this photograph

From 1875 all town councils had to provide regular road sweeping and rubbish collections. This photograph gives a good indication of how dirty the roads did become and the difficulty of sweeping them clean with a brush. Most street labourers were very poor.

Questions to ask

Why do streets need to be kept clean?

Points to explore

Buildings – type, features, materials.
Street – surface, appearance.

PHOTOGRAPH ON PAGE 23 **Construction of Warrington Bridge, 1913.**

About this photograph

An increase in traffic on both the roads and railways created problems and resulted in increased road building. The rubber pneumatic tyres of modern cars pulled stones up and the speed of the cars raised clouds of dust. Different types of street surfaces were experimented with, eventually resulting in what we have today.

Questions to ask

What materials are being used to make the bridge?
Why do you think a new road was being built?
How would it affect the people living near to it?

Points to explore

Clothing – hats, waistcoats, jackets, safety helmets.

PHOTOGRAPH ON PAGE 25 **Two Boys Lighting Gas Street Lamps, 1905.**

About this photograph

Before streets were lit by gas they had been lit by oil. The need to economise meant that it was usual for street lights to be off all summer and in many towns lights were turned off at midnight. By 1914 electric lighting was generally available but was used in several towns before that.

Questions to ask

What do you think the boys are doing?
What is the difference between this street light and the ones in your street?

Points to explore

Dangers involved in lighting lamps.
Different types of street lights in other photographs in the book.

PHOTOGRAPH ON PAGE 27 **Children at Play, National Playing Fields Appeal, 1919.**

About this photograph

This photograph was taken to illustrate the lack of play facilities for many children. Rapid house building in the nineteenth century had created many dwellings with no provision for gardens. The public parks of many towns and cities date from this period as an initial response to the need for open spaces. The children in the photograph seem quite oblivious to the photographer and are carrying on with turning the rope. The rope itself looks as though it is made up from scrap pieces of hemp used to tie parcels.

Questions to ask

What games are the children playing?
Why are they playing in the street?

Points to explore

Games to play which are free.
Clothing – hats, coats, shoes.
Street surfaces, furniture and buildings.

· Index ·

(Items that appear in text)